Little Blue Car Gets Lost

By: Nora Luke

Printed in USA

Published by: Nora Luke
© Copyright 2018

ISBN-10:

ISBN-13:

All Rights Reserved

No part of this publication may be reproduced

or transmitted in any form whatsoever, electronic,

or mechanical, including photocopying, recording,

or by any informational storage or retrieval system

without express written, dated and signed permission from the author.

By reading this you accept these terms and conditions.

Little Blue,
He felt so grown,
And often went out,
All alone.

His first drive,
Had caused alarm,
But he'd not come,
To any harm.

His mom said,
"I need to go,
To the store,
To shop," and so,

Little Blue said,
"I'll go there,"
His mom asked,
"Do you know where?"

"Oh yes,"he said,
I know the way,"
"Well if you're sure,"
His mom did say.

So to the store,
Drove Little Blue,
Certain what,
He had to do.

The way to go,
He thought he knew,
But soon got lost,
And upset too.

He was scared,
But then he saw,
A big truck,
Heading to the store.

Its name was written,
On the truck,
And Little Blue couldn't,
Believe his luck.

"Can I follow you,
To the store?"
He asked the truck,
Who said, "For sure."

So Little Blue,
He drove behind,
Until the store,
They both did find.

He bought the shopping,
And bags did pack,
But didn't know,
How to get back.

The truck said,
"Well, on this day,
I'll be driving,
Back that way.

You can follow,
Me again,
To your home,"
And so then,

That big truck,
And Little Blue,
Got back safe,
With the shopping too.

Little Blue knew,
On another day,
He'd take a map,
To find his way.

More book by: Nora Luke

Little Blue Car Gets Lost

Little Blue and Little Red

Little Blue car Big Race

Baby Bear Loves Candy

Baby Bear Doesn't Like the Dentist

Baby Bear Stays Up Too Late

Baby Bear Cleans His Room

About the Author

Nora Luke is a prolific children's author.
The 42-year-old children's fiction writer was born in Charlottesville, Virginia.
Drawing from her 15 years' experience in the field,
she has authored several children books which contribute immensely to their growth.

Her stories concentrate on the adventure
of floppy-eared bunnies and wide-eyed children learning lessons of life,

before returning home wiser and aching for sleep.
There's no limit to Nora's creativity as she sees beyond just writing good stories she incorporates
brilliant intuition and insight to make each piece of
her work unique and most importantly purposeful.

Disclaimer - Legal Notes

Every effort has been made to accurately
represent this book and it's potential.

Results vary with every individual, and your results may or may not
be different from those depicted.
No promises, guarantees or warranties,

whether stated or implied, have been made that you
will produce any specific result from this book.

Your efforts are individual and unique,
and may vary from those shown.

Your success depends on your efforts, background and motivation.
The author shall in no event be held liable
for any loss or other damages caused by

the use and misuse of or inability to
use any or all of the information described in this book.
By using the information in this book,

you agree to do so entirely at your own risk.
Use of the programs, advice,
and information contained in this

book is at the sole choice and risk of the reader.
Some website links referred to in this book

may be affiliate links and as such the author
will earn a commission on any purchases made.

Disclaimer - Legal Notes

Every effort has been made to accurately
represent this book and it's potential.

Results vary with every individual, and your results may or may not
be different from those depicted.
No promises, guarantees or warranties,

whether stated or implied, have been made that you
will produce any specific result from this book.

Your efforts are individual and unique,
and may vary from those shown.

Your success depends on your efforts, background and motivation.
The author shall in no event be held liable
for any loss or other damages caused by

the use and misuse of or inability to
use any or all of the information described in this book.
By using the information in this book,

you agree to do so entirely at your own risk.
Use of the programs, advice,
and information contained in this

book is at the sole choice and risk of the reader.
Some website links referred to in this book

may be affiliate links and as such the author
will earn a commission on any purchases made.

Lightning Source UK Ltd.
Milton Keynes UK
UKHW050952250621
386134UK00002B/104

9 789657 736364